Adopted

Abused

And Still

Standing

By:

Aleja Bennett

Bio of Aleja Bennett

Aleja Robbins (Bennett) was born in East Elmhurst Queens New York by her unknown biological mother. In 1976 she was raised in East New York Brooklyn by her church attending adopted parents who serve as a deacon and deaconess in the Victory Missionary Baptist Church. From the age of two through nineteen they physically, verbally, and mentally abused her. She was tortured, starved, made fun of, ridiculed and neglected all through her childhood.

Many nights she would cry leaving the pillows soaked and wet from crying all through the nights as a child. At the age of nine, she began to run away because it felt so safe being away from her adopted parents. She had a tidy room and a clean place to live so who would believe her? When she did confide in people they would go right behind her back and tell her parents.

She would get the worse beating ever for opening her mouth about what was really going on in the Robbins home. Fear was a major part of her childhood but when adulthood took over that fear started to disappear slowly. Aleja began to look for love in the wrong places with alcoholic and drug addicted men and their families. She didn't realize that these people would destroy and take her children in the long run.

Aleja was told to have an abortion at the age of nineteen or else she would be tossed to the cold, dark, and lonely streets of Brooklyn. When it was time for her to give her adopted parents an answer, Aleja stated that she will keep her baby. Her adopted father pushed her in the middle of her chest out of the project door in the cold of November without a coat, money, food or clothes. She was forced to live on her own with no where to call home.

Alcohol became a form of escape for her while she associated with people-men that added to her mental, emotional and physical abuse. At the age of twenty five while walking into her first A.A. meeting, she wrote her first poem titled Being Alive. From there she wrote eight titles,

Only the Strong Can Survive, Aleja's Beautiful Poetic Strategy in Recovery, Poems from the Heart Mind Body and Soul, Passions Desires of Aleja the Poet, Thoughts Deeply Rooted Within Me, Seasons With And Without Love, All I Can Do Is Stand, All I can Do Is Stand Part Two and Adopted Abused And Still Standing. Available on paper back and kindle on Amazon and other online book stores.

On March 27th 2011 after six weeks of attending Kingdom Life Ministries is when Aleja received her break through from God. Her joy and passion for singing was restored as the Holy Spirit began to deal with her by knocking her down to her knees. Pastor David Yankana asked her to sing His Eye Is On the Sparrow. While singing this powerful song was when Aleja started to feel the joy, power and anointing in her voice.

The entire church caught the Holy Ghost that day and Aleja's life would now take a turn for the better. She now records singing videos on you tube with a live recorded testimony of how her life has changed. She also has written two songs titled All I Can DO Is Stand and Stand Up For Life which were written in January 2011. She plans to have them recorded by an already recorded gospel group.

Aleja Bennett has started a choir at Kingdom Life Ministries named Kingdom Reign. She works with the choir faithfully, lovingly, kindly and patiently every Wednesday for rehearsal. For her, singing to God is a form of release from all the pain that she had to endure including all the things she has lost. The past has always hurt Aleja in some kind of way so now she can't trust the people from it because it has slowed her down.

As the choir progresses there seems to be so much negative comments about them singing off key. It's very hard to find people to work with you as easy as it is for them to work against you. I told a choir member that if someone tells you that you're off key, just walk away because I don't want to hear anything negative. While training the choir it is up to me to make sure that they are all on key. My prayer is that God will send me a fire filled, anointed musician that can play all the songs that we can sing.

In life nothing is easy no matter how sincere you are about it. There will always be one to have something negative to say about the positive things that you are doing. I really receive great joy from working with the choir each week and hearing their voices becoming stronger and stronger. When praises are being lifted up to God it can't help but to be blessed.

I came to Kingdom Life Ministries stating that I would never sing again. Instead I tried my best to hide behind the choir by training their voices. It seemed as if the joy of singing was swiped away from me. There no longer was that joy from singing that was once a major part of me.

The people from my past left many wounds wide open, it seemed as if they just left me for dead. When the children were taken it ripped the joy from underneath my soul. Only a real God could bring such joy back into a depressed, broken, hurting soul such as Aleja Bennett. My dream is to have an organization, Teen Speak Out all over the world as it will be a safe haven for ages twelve to twenty. This will be a safe haven where teenagers can enjoy indoor and outdoor activity in a safe, drug and alcohol free environment. It would prevent teenage pregnancy, abuse and abandonment.

Aleja writes not just to share her story but to empower, strengthen, and encourage people all over the world. Her mission has been to lift up the depressed, broken, wounded, injured, sad, addicted, abuse victims, teens and adopted children all over the world. Adopted children have it so hard these days because most of us have never seen or will never see our birth parents or siblings. To this day I have yet to meet any of my biological family. Today many are being adopted and not genuinely being loved and cared for. To many adopted parents it is all about that check that comes in their mail box. They will fix up their apartments and have the children looking like trash.

Adopted children are being abused, mistreated and neglected as well. They have to face all that, plus not knowing who they belong to. What a horrible way to start out a child's life by not knowing their true identity. These books are intended for the sole purpose of building lives that have been torn down, abused and rejected.

Her writing helps so many people as it allows her healing to process faster. Aleja's main goal is to stop the form of abuse or at least give people a desire to no longer deal with it. She writes for all ages excluding some of the romance poems that might not be suitable for certain ages. The majority of her works are for all ages to read.

Aleja Bennett has started an organization all over the world called Teen Speak Out where teens always have a safe place to speak their mind and receive any services they may need for their immediate situation. Teens and adults can follow her blogs below.

http://alejabennett.blogspot.com
http://stopabusewithaleja.blogspot.com

http://bestbooks2read.blogspot.com

http://gospelwithaleja.blogspot.com

This last blogs are for those that want to keep their

Day jobs but make a little extra cash with these well

Known companies listed on the money blog.

http://moneyfor2011.blogspot.com

Teen Speak Out is for Teens between the ages of twelve through twenty only. This will be to stop the cycle of abuse-drugs-runaways-teen pregnancy and loneliness due to hard working parents or parent's addicted to drugs. Her vision for this started due to her running away from the age of nine to the unsafe streets. However she survived but unfortunately many others are not so fortunate. The streets are filled with gangs, drugs, prostitution and violence.

Teen Speak Out will keep our teens off the streets in a clean safe, positive, learning environment. A place where they can speak out, learn, share and set long and short term goals for

their lives. Her pay pal account is
aleja_bennett@yahoo.com Please donate so that
she can rent or buy her first building and expand
it nation wide.

Face Book http://www.facebook.com/pages/Aleja-Bennett/174745539242473

You can order all nine books on paper back and
kindle on Amazon.

Now at the age of thirty eight Aleja still continues to write words that uplift and help so many around her and over the internet. She has become a motivational speaker, a poet, an author, a singer and an all-around good friend if you need one. You can join both her fan pages on Face book which displays her books, videos and inspirational messages. Let her know if you want her to come to your town, church or function.

Aleja doesn't just try to sale books, it's the message that is in the books that she so desires to be delivered. All are touching, empowering, strengthening, and uplifting. Instead of feeling powerless: be inspired, motivated, healed and learn the method of forgiveness to the offender.

In this life the very people that we trust, forgive and love will be the people that will cause us so much hurt and despair. If we are not careful it could destroy our lives. My Pastor taught us about forgiveness and how it is important to forgive the offender. I refuse to be a victim by people that have left me for dead, broken, wounded and sad.

Only God has kept me in this unfair society where lies rule by separating families. Who separates a mother, son and daughters? The very people that we have tried to rid from our lives will be the ones to take all you have when you're not even aware of it.

I couldn't believe how all three of my children loved to be around people that didn't like me or care for our relationship. These people didn't stop until they manipulated them against me. There was no family standing by my side to fight for me and my children.

I always had to go up against the enemy all alone. In the end I was defeated by lies that led me to walk. Well at least this is what I thought until the power of a praying church took over.

Message from The Author

The books that I've been writing are short and straight to the point. They are written so that the reader can go back to that specific page and catch a glimpse of strength. I choose not to write lengthy books because what I have to say is summed up with pain, struggle then triumph. It doesn't take a long book to change your way of thinking from negative to a positive.

The books that I have read in my life were always shorter than mine. It gave me what I needed which was a quick pick me up. Allow my books to give you that as well. You can keep the books down through the years and pass them off to your off spring. The words that are written were made to linger on your mind way after you have finished reading them.

Remember it is not about how many pages that a book has but what the book has inside of it. What was the message to you? Did it make you cry? Was it something that was shared that you could relate to? After reading the books did it change your life in a positive way? Was the message you received loud and clear?

I write because it started the healing process of abuse, rejections and pain in my life. I have survived some terrible, unfair ordeals and many others have chosen suicide as the way out. Many abuse victims have been murdered by their abusers. If I write lengthy books that suicidal person might just get in a hurry to finish what they are thinking.

If I leave my books short and straight to the point then that suicidal mind would think twice about ending his or her life. They will see quickly how I have survived without knowing my parents, siblings and through the abuse of alcohol, separation from my three children and how I still remain standing.

It is not about how many pages that I write. It has been all about me saving lives from depression, abuse and open wounds that are still bleeding. I want you to bleed no more because while you continue to bleed, the person or people that cut you are still cutting others. They are living their lives as if they have done nothing wrong to you.

Why can't you go on living your life with the joy of helping others survive? We all can help each other rise up out of this pit of depression and suicidal thinking. Teach someone else to live instead of throwing the towel in. That way is too quick and God does not forgive you for taking your own life. We do not have that right or say so.

It is he who made you and for a purpose. Share your new strength, story and past experiences with another victim of abuse and watch how your life starts to turn around. Let them know what books to read from one survivor to the next. Together we can heal a hurting world of people. Take that same pain and use it for your gifts, talents and the well being of others.

Share with me your stories on my fan pages Aleja Bennett and Author Aleja Bennett on face book. I look forward to reading all about your life change and how you are taking that pain and turning it into triumph, glory for the Lord.

No weapon formed against me or you shall prosper for we are more than conquerors. I was glad when they said unto me let us go into the house of the Lord. When my mother and father forsake me then the Lord will take me up. Sing unto the Lord a new song sing unto the Lord all the earth. Let all the people praise thee let all the people praise thy name forever and forever more. The title of this book is to let the readers know about a life of struggle, pain, abuse, rejection to becoming a woman of strength.

In all that we have gone through in this life there should be a better, positive outcome. Many take their own lives because the pain is too hard to bear from the past and present trauma experiences. We want to give up instead of finding out what our sole purpose is for even being alive.

If people are trying to take you out then you must really be an important person. You have a destiny that someone doesn't want to blossom out and grow. It is hard to pursue who we are meant to be after enduring so many terrible incidents. We find it so unbearable to stand while the tears constantly roll down our cheeks while people walk out of our lives that we love.

We have invested time, money and a genuine concern for the ones that have been placed in our path and it hurts when they turn on us. You feel as if your time and life has been wasted with these people when you could have been devoted, loving and caring for other people that would cherish it.

The very familiar words that have been said to us all from someone we love, Trust me I love you and will never hurt you. Those words stick so close and tight within us all. After we start to trust them slowly we start to see them for who they really are as time goes by. The very same people that you thought would never hurt you will one day be a shocking surprise to you. Place your trust in God alone because his genuine love for us never leaves us or fails. God can't and wont be manipulated to turn against you ever.

Adopted

Abused

And

Still

Standing

By: Aleja Bennett

Special Thanks

I have to thank God for keeping my mind, body and health through all the pain and suffering in my life. God has been keeping me all these years through the ups downs and merry go rounds of my life. I'm not perfect and never will be but I have a heart of gold that is genuine once I trust a person.

To Kingdom Life Ministries with Pastor David Yankana and his wife Angie Yankana. My spiritual mom Fazia Rahaman, Joan Norbath, Sabrina Smith, Nora Ali, Larrion Fenlator. My life changed once I walked into the doors of this church.

They have been praying for me over the phone and privately. Things started to happen with my books and the enemy became very busy. Through the continuous prayers of mom and Kingdom Life Ministries enabled positive changes in my life today. I'm truly blessed to belong to a church such as this. We are located in Richmond Hill NY.

Lucan is still a major part of my life and through being ill for a couple of weeks he was the one who nursed me back to health. We may not always agree because we are both set in our own ways but he is so very appreciated by me. I would like to take this time to thank Lucan for putting up with a spoiled brat like me.

To the entire Create Space, Amazon, Borders Express Book Store, Sister's

Uptown Book Store, and thanks for allowing my books to be signed.

A special thanks to my daughter Jessica P. Robbins for her dedication to furthering her education at The Lawrence University College.

We have reunited as mother and daughter since 5/2/11

She has now published her first book with my help, titled The Creative Mind of A Poet by Jessica P. Robbins on Amazon paper back and kindle.

http://createspace.com/3607675

Her second book now out

The Easy Way Out

http://createsoace.com/3609635

A Mother

A mother who wasn't perfect

A mother who had that genuine love

A mom who would go without

A mother who wanted them to have

A mom who played with her young

A mother who fed and kept them safe

A mom who nursed them back to health

A mother who was strict about education

A mom who kept them well fed

A mother who would watch them as they slept

A mom who allowed them to play in her bed

A mother who breast fed her young

A mom that took you to exquisite restaurants

A mother who would rock you to sleep

A mom who would sing you to sleep

A mother who would write songs that we would sing

A mom who was proud and gave praise when they were excellent

A mother who taught independence

A mom who wanted the best for them

A mother who had to finally let go

A mother who had to finally smell
the roses

A mom who needed peace after being
ignored

A mother who has been separated
while they go on, she too must go on.

Adopted Abused and Still Standing

Children often forget where they have come from especially by the woman that gave them life. I don't seem to understand or never will understand why a child would live with a crack head, in the projects that sniffs cocaine and drinks like a fish.

How could a child leave their own mother for this type of person? Why must children leave a clean environment with plenty of food and shelter for the life of the projects? This is something that really puzzles me. I have never abused my children or neglected them in anyway.

There are children out there that wish a mother like me could be in their lives today. Many of them have been starved, beaten, neglected, tortured and put through horrific measures. A mother is never perfect but there is no one that will genuinely love you like the one who nursed you in your cradle.

Right in my neighborhood there are several children living in unclean conditions, no food and smelling very bad. These women still have their kids because no one that is related to them would dare take their kids away.

These people don't have money hungry kid takers, in their lives as I do. I must admit that by sleeping with three different African

American men, making children by them was a mistake that I'm dearly paying for today.

Not one of the fathers financially supported their children due to drugs, alcohol, women, jail and lies. These men are able to be around my children and I'm told to stay away. Is this really happening? This must be a dream that Aleja has not waken up from yet. My ex husband had told me to forget about Arthea. This is the reason why I date foreign men because my own people have taken away everything from me.

They all have walked away thinking that I am dead. Sorry fellows Aleja is still standing, alive, well and kicking. If it was not for the Lord in my heart, soul and mind then jail would have been a life sentence for me.

My ex-husband is allowed to spend most of his life in jail and still have a relationship with his daughter while I can't. His sister has my seven year old son and sixteen year old daughter. She sniffs cocaine, drinks alcohol while three children sleep in the same bedroom.

When I explained this to children services all they did was tell me that this was not true. No matter what I told this worker it would go in one of her ears and out of the next one. For some reason I never could win against crack heads because they need money to keep up with that expensive habit.

Arthea no longer participates in church as she use to when she resided with me. She sang on the choir and was a member of the usher board and girl scouts.

It really hurt me to know that she no longer attends church and was kicked out of the performing arts school for fighting. She now attends a school that I'm not fond of but if she is doing well as she stated then I am very proud of her.

It surprises me to see that people will use your very own kids in order to have the financial compensation for them to buy drugs and furniture. What is this world coming to when these type of things start to happen? If it was not for the fear of the Lord that was placed in me then,

I could have taken everyone out that has injured my inner soul and being. I'm not that type of person but I do know that you all will pay for what you have done to me as you have already started paying.

Every time someone dies in your family think about the times when you stole my children. When you are sick from the alcohol and drugs you take just remember that you stole my children. When God decides to rack your body with pain, just remember that you stole a loving mother's children.

It only takes a mighty God to keep my mind from insanity. That is where the poetry had come from. It really kept me standing through all the painful memories of my life. I remember how the agency thought that I was a crack head when they saw me because of the lies that were told.

She didn't realize that Aleja was a diva, an attractive woman that many are jealous of. The same woman that stole my children felt uncomfortable with her cheating man around me, talk about insecurity!

Often the life that I have lived really enables me to think that I'm only dreaming no! This can't have happened to me! God can you bless me with a do over life? How many of us would like to start over? Many of us would prefer to live poor then travel back in time of abusive childhood memories.

I was the mother that rocked and sang you to sleep. A mother that made sure you had the best education. You have had a mom that would jump, run and play with you as if she was a kid too. My kids have had a mom that taught them how to cook.

I was a mom that would run to the school every time the teacher would call. Aleja was a mother who made sure that they went to the doctor. My children had a mom that kept the house and clothes cleaned. If I had money in my pocket then there was nothing that I wouldn't buy for them.

There were many times when Arthea was given one hundred dollars in her pocket on pay day while working as a security guard. All three of my children are not in my life today but I remain living, breathing and standing. Arthea doesn't get hundred dollar bills anymore living with her auntie.

I was a mother who would write songs and sang them to my children. I was a mom who breast fed all three but only the boy would take the breast milk. I was a mom that took her children to French, Italian and Spanish restaurants in the city.

I was a mother who liked to have some drinks and often Arthea would be the one to drain me dry out of my pockets at those times. While drinking she too wanted to drink and many times she would sneak and do it behind my back.

I was the type of mother that often allowed my children to walk all over me. There were many times that I had to run to the school for Arthea being nosy and into fights. I would always tell her that gossip is nothing but trouble. I had to remain standing even when my children wouldn't listen to me.

They are aware that there was a time when I would give up my life to safe theirs. I was the mom who allowed her children to sleep in the bed with her. I was a mom who would watch them play fight with each other while jumping all over my bed.

Where can most children find a mom like that? There are not too many of us out there today. I was a mom who went without clothes and shoes so they could have. I was a mom who would silently cry at night because of disobedience.

I was a mom who wanted the best schools, environment and places for them. I was that mother that played in the snow with them. Many time they brought out that inner child within me. They allowed me to often be a child right along with them. Due to my childhood being taken from me, my children gave me a childhood to remember. It's a sad world when the day comes when children do not wake up wanting or missing their own mother.

Foster care has been dishing out money to crack heads in the projects to take care of your children. This is a crying shame and a pity. When I inquired about a drug test for the person that stole my children, she told them that she was on her cycle.

When she finally took the test her system was cleaned out from a product that she took. This woman sniffs cocaine, her boyfriend and most of her whole family and friends. This is the unsafe environment where my two children are residing.

It is time that I let the world know what has happened to me. When drug addicts start to con the children protective services then there is a major problem. Children are no longer safe anymore in the system. Many are beaten, injured, molested, raped, alcoholics, runaways and prostitutes.

It has been very unbearable to live knowing that two of my children are living in unsafe conditions. Due to God coming into my life on Sunday March 27, 2011 started a serious life change for me. The painful incidents that had happened in my life felt like no more.

The joy of the Lord has come over me after singing his eye is on the sparrow. I had told myself that there was nothing for me to sing about. God enabled me to feel his love, joy and concern over my life. God had been my joy all along and here I was depressed, lonely, sad and drinking.

It's something about holding that microphone in my hands that has a strong hold over me. Have I found my peace, joy and comfort? Yes. I have found it resting and trusting in Jesus, who is the sweetest man that I know.

Once I allowed God to come in day by day he started to clean my mind, heart, body and soul. He kept me alive for a reason because there is a work that I must do for the Lord and I am no longer ashamed of my calling.

Through the years of my life there were times when I would write a poem, song or even thought of writing a play. It was now time that the talent's given to me had started to unfold and come to pass.

Singing always gave me such a great joy and a feeling of release from all negative moments in the past that would haunt me.

Here we go into another new year 2011. I'm praying that the world that God created stays the same and that the people inside of it take a stand for change. He made such a beautiful earth for us to dwell in and so many of us are taking that for granted. Why? Have we forgotten that Jesus took a stand for all of us by dying on the cross?

Will we take a stand by letting go of all the anger that builds up on the insides of us? Will we finally take a stand to love others just as he loves us? Why do we stand for holding childhood grudges into our adult lives? Will we ever move and live at peace with such a terrible past?

We can live at peace because God gave us the power to do so in his word. As I look back over my life then look inside of it now, the scriptures are revealing itself. Often we become impatient thinking that the bible is a lie. If you can just hold on for a little while the bible will come to pass in your life. When it does happen what will you do or say? How will you feel? Will you then believe? Growing up as an unwanted adopted child was very painful.

It was a life filled with mistreatment-neglect and sadness. Sitting in the corner was a place where my childhood was spent. Being out of the way probably kept me safe for a little while at least. While every one mingled downstairs there I was upstairs all alone.

I use to wait for the days to be picked up or even held but those days never happened. It's funny how even as an adult I still waited for that real genuine hug, kiss just love. If we don't receive attention-warmth and love as a child then we look for it as an adult. We tend to find it in the worst places such as the bars and club scene.

Once the sober bells kick off we begin to find out who this character really is. Many times it is someone that we want no parts of. We wanted this person to be the one to give us this love we've been so desperately waiting for. In trust we thought that not all people can be bad so let's give it a chance.

Someone was always telling me to give a person a chance right after my heart was broken numerous of times. Now I know to give my heart a break to feel relief from the brokenness. I knew that I had the power to stand through all the false relationships that I was engaged in. It felt like someone was stabbing me in the chest each time someone walked out.

It was very hard for me to leave once falling in love came into play. All I wanted was to be by myself but the devil would say I'm not going to hurt you all I want to do is love you. Wow! Men are really slick they know the lines to say that will make you fall weak at the knees. As I became older it finally started to sink in that these men were not what I wanted in my life.

I figured older men would be the safest to tangle up with but they were the same as anybody else. They would leave you before you could even think about leaving them. Every heart break would send me to the bars where loneliness would kick in. I tried to hide the pain and sorrow but the tears would send me running to the bathroom.

As a little girl the bathroom kept the secrets of my many shredded tears. As an adult when the tears would start to roll I would roll of right to the bathroom mirror. This was a place where my tears were between the mirror and I alone. This was a little secret that was kept for years. Even as an adult I find myself still going to the bathroom mirror watching the tears as they fall down to my lips.

Often this would take me back to childhood memory lane. The mirror allowed me to see the pain-blood and swollen lips from abuse. The bath room mirror also allowed me to see the sorrow in my eyes. I saw sadness-fear and low self esteem in the bath room mirror. Eventually I didn't want anyone to cause this pain in my life anymore.

I had to take a stand on who was healthy to be in my life. If the person was healthy for me then there is no way he or she would hurt me. There are times when I'm faced with the question, should I allow this person or that one to enter into my life?

 It can be confusing especially when they seem so nice in the beginning. Before I can make a decision they are already gone. I'm sort of glad that they are finally seeing that I'm not a push over or someone that they can use for personal gain.

Before I can say hit the road now they are already gone. I sure wish that I would have taken the time to know people better before it caused me everything. Through the years it was so easy to let someone in rather than let them out. Standing through so many unbelievable circumstances has been very hard but the more you stand the stronger you will become. I've been abused, neglected, rejected, homeless, jobless, motherless, fatherless, broken hearted and separated from my children and I'm still standing. These were the toughest battles in my life.

Do I give up and throw the towel in? Do I live through it and stand without a scratch? I chose to stand with the tears as time will erase some of that pain. It sure has dried up the tears for incidents that I once cried over. I'm no longer shedding tears for any of those reasons today.

When you choose to live that means you chose to stand through all the daggers that are coming your way. Don't think that a terrible storm can't hit your way again. It can come from any angle even on the internet. I had to back away from a place where someone always wanted something and it was taking the focus off my books. I was supporting and not receiving that same support. People will stick under you just for you to be a service to them. A donation-a purchase and meanwhile you are not selling one thing.

You became too busy helping others succeed instead of keeping the focus on your own product. Every day can be such a learning experience whether you leave the house or on the internet. I found myself having to take a stand by finding other avenues to promote all my books.

In January around the beginning of the month is when I started to feel pain in my right leg. The pain started to increase severely to where it was time for medical attention. I reached for the phone and called my friend Sheryl as she was too busy staying at home doing nothing at all. The ambulance had to come for me because I could not walk at all. The pain was excruciating to where it brought constant tears to my eyes. My boyfriend suggested for me to go due to him being unable to leave work.

By the time I reached to the hospital I decided to give my so called best friend one last call. This was a moment in my life when I started to feel all alone with this terrible agonizing pain in my right leg. Make a long story short and brief, she never showed up to the hospital.

I was released with pain killers and was treated very badly by the staff in the Jamaica Hospital in Queens New York. All I could do was cry as the pain constantly struck me. When you arrive to the emergency room all alone they treat you any kind of way. What happened to people really loving and caring about their work? Now I see that it is just a pay check and how I had to stand through the pain and mistreatment from the nurses.

When it was time for the sonogram everywhere the lady touched the leg would cause me to cry. She caught an attitude and never finished the procedure. Rolled my bed out and parked it against the wall as if I was an animal.

Wow! This was really a test of strength on my part. Should I punch this woman across her face? Or should I just stand in the midst of all the wrongness that's being done? I did not touch any of those nurses. God knows that I really wanted to show them the pain that I was feeling.

Two wrongs don't make a right, beside it would have made matters a whole lot worse for me. Often we think it will feel so good just to punch someone's lights out for the evil things they do. I'm not even going to say that people don't deserve it. Leave it to God he will take care of them.

We will reap what we sow for the evil plots we do in this life. The pain increased for two weeks after that horrific hospital visit. Lucan was taking care of me from day to day. He was the only one that was taking care of me as if he was my husband.

He even asked what happened to all your friends including my best friend Sheryl. Not one friend came and showed up for one second. The pain seemed to be getting worse day by day, even with muscle relaxers and pain killers.

It was now time to go to a clinic for an x-ray to see what was really going on inside of my body. Lucan continued to bring me food, muscle relaxers and massage my body down. I really thank God for sending him into my life.

The doctor informed me that I had a herniated disk in my back and it's affecting my right leg. What a relief! I now know what is wrong with me and can do what the doctor says to heal it.

Physical therapy was needed in order to straighten my back enabling me to stop limping. Through all the pain that was afflicted upon me with no friends around I still remained standing.

I wrote two songs while I was racked with pain. All I Can Do Is Stand and Stand Up For Life. These songs are so powerful and I can't believe that in all that pain Aleja began to write songs that will uplift the nation. These songs really gave me such a spiritual awakening. It just amazes me how God works and dwells in me even through physical pain.

I already know what singing group I want to minister these songs, Kirk Franklin and the family. Maybe he will get a copy of this book and find this information out. Spiritual music always empowers me to stand even more. It gives us the strength to go at it with life once more.

For about seven to eight years I have lived in Richmond Hill NY. The stores have received a pretty penny from me down through then years. I decided to make them aware that I'm an Author and that my books are available for sale.

The books were shown to the store owners; which they didn't purchase not one of the eight books that were shown to them. The only person that bought one was the woman at the liquor store. She was very shocked to hear that the other stores in the neighborhood didn't support me.

Isn't this quite weird how the woman at the wine store bought a book and no one else did? Maybe I was buying too much liquor there at one time. Many times we give up on a dream allowing others to make that call for us why? God gave you and I a gift and we are to use it to the utmost ability.

Through rejections we stand

Through lies we stand

Through non supporters we stand

Through jealousy we stand

Through writing, singing, acting,

Preaching, teaching we stand.

When doors are closed all around
you time after time again I'm asking
you to just be silent walk away and
stand. Before you know it quietly and
often very quickly another door
opens to stay open. One day I guess
when we least expect it the blessings
will flow in all of our lives.

It's sad to see so many women
including myself ripped away from
their children especially when I see
so many of them neglected. With my
own eyes as well as many of us have
see children residing in filthy
apartments, hair uncombed and with
little or no food.

The type of mother that I was to my children was nothing like that. They were manipulated away from me by a drug addict. Now after looking over my life, there were many manipulators just waiting for the chance to take everything that I had. It has always been extremely hard for me to accomplish a singing career and the sale of my books. It was as if someone or something was placing a block over my life.

Every time Aleja took a stand for the gifts that God gave me I was simply in third place. It was and still is very hard for me to understand why did God give me a voice that people were so jealous of? If Aleja didn't remain standing where would I be today?

The same people that have been hurting me all my life seemed to have left me for dead. I'm still here and it's so shocking because all the lies and the manipulations that were sought out still has Aleja standing.

Each time a person walked out of my life I would head straight to the bottle. Alcohol became a pain reliever from all the deceivers that wouldn't go away until they took everything that I had. If they really cared about me they would have seen the pain that I was in.

A yearning to be loved and to receive love was all I ever wanted. The love and forgiveness in my heart always kept me going strong. Love was something that was so easy for me to give. It's apart of who I am and the type of mother I was. I kept all three of them clean, safe, fed and warm. Today is a new day and as I write of all the sadness and pain Aleja has some joy in her life. Due to my oldest daughter being injured at college became an open door, bond for mother and child to come together.

God will work in the most mysterious way in order for us to see the real genuine love that a mother has for you. After all the false truths at this new age she can see that her mom truly loves her and I really do with all my heart.

It's a shame that we live in a world where people will tear children apart from their mother but that child must grow up one day and will be able to make the choice for themselves. Often they have to be far away from the area that they had been residing. Love made me travel thirty something hours on the greyhound bus to Appleton, Wisconsin. It was so nice to see my first born and to see how well she had been doing in college.

Jessica is well liked in her school by many different cultures and that makes me smile. I always wanted my children to be around different cultures so that they can learn new and different things. She is embarking on a journey that I have always dreamed of for all my children. I just want the best for them and they know that education has always been something I have taken seriously.

Being on campus with my daughter was definitely an unforgettable experience. We finally got the chance to bond, talk, and break all the barriers standing in our way. We got the chance to sing together like we used to. We got the chance to have coffee at Starbucks and chat: a gesture so small means so much when you have been away from your child for so long. It was definitely worth it and I enjoyed being there for her and with her.

While drinking coffee, Jessica and I thought of doing an event on campus for me, my story, and an opportunity to motivate other students and faculty. We put together a "Meet The Author" event on May 8th, 2011 in Kohler Hall

Lounge. Her friends got together and set up and created programs. It was on Mother's Day. It was by far, one of the best Mother's Days for me.

www.ingramcontent.com/pod-product-compliance
Lightning Source LLC
Chambersburg PA
CBHW071244280526
45788CB00004B/1579